Old CAMPBELTOWN and MACH

by
Carol McNeill

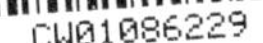

The fine selection of headgear – from the ladies' elaborate hats to the gentlemen's bowlers and toppers – together with the horse-drawn brakes, suggests that this view of Main Street was taken on a holiday. The last, four-storey, building pictured on the left-hand side was Lloyd's Hotel – 'week-enders and golfers specially catered for' – with Johnston's public house on the street level. The hotel's owners later bought the neighbouring piece of ground (surrounded by a wall in the picture) to build the imposing Royal Hotel, which was completed in 1907.

The White Hart Hotel has been in a commanding position at the top of Main Street since Georgian times. Its distinctive corner tower was added when the building was remodelled in 1897. A local guidebook of 1907 listed its attractions, which included being '... replete with every modern convenience. Electric Bells throughout. Telephones to Hotel Office on all landings. Boots attend all steamers.' Golfers were specially catered for, with special terms for 'commercial gentlemen'. Terms then were £2 5/- for weekly board and 15/6d for the weekend. The white hart or stag in the picture was removed many years ago, but a new version was mounted on the wall of the hotel in 2003.

First published in the United Kingdom, 2004,
reprinted 2007, 2009
by Stenlake Publishing Ltd.,
01290 551122
www.stenlake.co.uk

ISBN 9781840332926

FURTHER READING

The books listed below were used by the author during her research. None of them are available from Stenlake Publishing. Those interested in finding out more are advised to contact their local bookshop or reference library.

Argyllshire Herald archives.
Campbeltown Courier archives.
Campbeltown records held in Argyll & Bute County Archives, Lochgilphead.
Kintyre Civic Society, *The Campbeltown Book*, 2003.
Nigel Macmillan, *The Campbeltown and Machrihanish Light Railway*, 1970.
Angus Martin, *The Ring-Net Fishermen*, 1981; *The North Herring Fishing*, 2001; *Herring Fishermen of Kintyre and Ayrshire*, 2002.
Machrihanish SWRI Village History Book, 1966.
Picturesque Campbeltown, Southend and Machrihanish Guidebook, 1907.

ACKNOWLEDGEMENTS

In particular, I would like to thank Angus Martin, who gave so generously of his time and tremendous depth of knowledge, and for the use of the photographs which appear on pages 13, 28 and 29. Thanks are also due to Robert Douglas (Australia); Jane Gallagher (Campbeltown); David MacArthur; James Macdonald (Campbeltown); Machrihanish SWRI; Murdo MacDonald, Argyll & Bute Council archivist; Archie McNicol (Campbeltown); George and Margaret McSporran (Campbeltown); Margaret and Jim Millar (Campbeltown); Bob Smith (Linlithgow); Jim Swan (Dysart); Marion Plenderleith (Lincolnshire) for permission to use the photograph on page 47; Olive Lees (Glasgow) for the photograph on page 39 (upper); and Eric Simpson (Dalgety Bay) for the photograph on page 46. I would like to dedicate this book to the memory of my father and mother, John and Nancy Burgess, who would, I think, have approved.

The photographs on pages 2, 8 (flood), 14, 36, 39 (comic), 41, 42, 43 (Gauldrons) and the inside back cover come from the author's collection, while the back cover photograph comes from the publishers' collection. The publishers wish to thank Emslie and Ian MacPherson who provided the remaining photographs in the book.

INTRODUCTION

Campbeltown, which is situated near the southern end of the peninsula of Kintyre, is a Lowland mainland town which still manages to have the atmosphere of an island community – and a Highland one at that. With a current population of around 5,000, it has been called the most southerly part of the Highlands, but it is in fact further south than Berwick. Thanks to the influence of the Gulf Stream, the climate is comparatively balmy; deep snow is rarely seen except in the harshest winters, and palm trees flourish on the Prom.

Because of its remoteness and given the hilly and loch-indented terrain of Argyll, getting to Campbeltown from almost anywhere can never be in a straight line; drivers accustomed to motorways are surprised at the time it takes to cover the 140 miles from Glasgow. In the not too distant past, the easiest and certainly most pleasant method of reaching Campbeltown was by steamer, but the *Davaar*, *Kinloch*, *Kintyre*, *Queen Alexandra* and *King Edward* are now only memories. Even the grand old lady of comparatively recent times, the *Duchess of Hamilton*, the last regular steamer to visit the town, no longer ties up at the Old Quay to set visitors and locals ashore and to provide a focal point to the afternoon. There has never been a national rail network between Campbeltown and the rest of the world. However, there was a local railway service in the short-lived but romantically remembered narrow-gauge Campbeltown & Machrihanish Light Railway. It started running a passenger service in 1906, travelling from the Quay head terminus with its track laid along the public highway in the middle of Hall Street, and ending its five-mile journey in Machrihanish. A favourite with tourists and natives alike, it came to the end of its tracks in 1932.

The town grew from a centuries-old tiny settlement called *Ceann-Loch-Chille-Ciaran* ('the head of the loch of the church of Ciaran'). To its inhabitants and friends, however, it's more affectionately known simply as the 'Wee Toon'.

It received its Royal Burgh Charter on 19 April 1700, a document which gave authority to Archibald Campbell, tenth Earl of Argyll, to appoint the first town council with its provost, bailies, dean of guild, treasurer and 12 councillors; it also led to the building of the impressive Town Hall in 1760.

The area is rich in archaeology and ancient reminders of times past. Various Bronze Age burial cists, yielding pottery vessels, tools and jewellery, have been unearthed in sites such as Trench Point and Glenramskill. The most important discovery was in 1970, when a magnificent jet necklace and matching bracelet were found near the former avenue into Stronvaar House. The 113-bead necklace, made of Whitby jet and considered to be one of the finest ever found, is on permanent display in Campbeltown Museum.

Singer Andy Stewart's popular song 'Campbeltown Loch, I wish you were whisky' has a ring of truth about it, as in the 1830s there were more than 30 distilleries operating in the town. Whisky continues to be made by the two remaining distilleries, Springbank and Glen Scotia, and whisky connoisseurs are highly appreciative of their single malts and blends.

The town's other economic mainstays over the years have been fishing (with its associated industries of rope- and net-making), shipbuilding, mining, farming and tourism. Over the past few years, business and factory closures have increased the already high unemployment rate; and although a ferry link with Northern Ireland was inaugurated in 1997 with an extension to the New Quay, the service was short-lived and is currently not in operation. The herring fishing has long gone, but a greatly depleted fleet still brings in shellfish, including a very large type of prawn, the Norway lobster, which is now its mainstay.

Dalintober, now an accepted part of the town, was a separate fishing community until the late nineteenth century. It had its own quay, fishing fleet, shops and pubs, and for the brave souls who wished to make the journey there was even a ferry which ran between Dalintober Quay and Cambeltown's Old Quay. In the late 1880s, the sea at the head of the loch (the Mussell Ebb) was filled in to make Kinloch Park, and the two communities were then within easy walking distance.

Campbeltown has produced many famous sons (and daughters), particularly in the nineteenth century, with many men of distinction in various fields making a worldwide mark. For instance, Sir William MacKinnon of Balinakill and Strathaird, born in Campbeltown in 1823, founded the British East India Company. Captains of industry included David Colville, iron and steel manufacturer and founder of David Colville and Sons of Motherwell, and James Templeton, whose carpet factory in Glasgow provided floor coverings for generations of homes. William McTaggart RSA (1835–1910), born on the farm of Aros just outwith Campbeltown and brought up in the town, got inspiration for many of his most beautiful paintings around the beaches of Machrihanish, while artist Archibald McKinnon painted his vision of the Crucifixion in a cave on Davaar Island, at the mouth of Campbeltown Loch, in 1887.

Five miles away from Campbeltown, across the flat Laggan of Kintyre, lies Machrihanish, set on the shores of the ever-changing Atlantic with miles of golden sand, two renowned golf courses, lush farmland and breathtaking scenery which includes the islands of Jura and Islay and (on a clear day) Rathlin off the Irish coast.

Just before the start of the twentieth century, Machrihanish consisted of just a small row of cottages to the west of the present village. This was known as the Pans, Saltpans or Mary Pans, after the salt-making industry which went on there. It was predominantly a farming community, with some fishing carried out by a few families. For leisure, there was the golf course which was laid out in 1876, with the Ugadale Arms Hotel and several boarding houses to cater for visitors. In 1893, the first villa was built and a row of impressive houses followed, as well as the Mission Hall, a post office, and a village general store.

Argyll Colliery at West Trodigal (less than a mile from Machrihanish), which was an important source of employment over the years, closed its doors in March 1967, and the site is now a holiday caravan park. The RAF and NATO airbase, where Concorde and the American Stealth bomber were tested, is now effectively redundant and the military housing turned over for civilian occupation.

However, the airport still provides quick links with Glasgow, and tourists from other parts of Scotland and abroad delight in getting away from it all to enjoy the local whisky, beef, lamb, seafood and cheeses, as well as the hospitality of the local people.

The unique atmosphere, settings and rich history, combined with a strong sense of community, make Campbeltown and the surrounding area a very special place in the hearts and minds of all those who are proud to have connections with the 'Wee Toon'.

This postcard, sent in 1910, shows a busy view of Main Street, looking towards Castlehill and dominated by the fine Town Hall which was built in 1760. Its original wooden spire was replaced by a stone one in 1778. Shop fronts visible include (on the right) Daniel Paterson, watchmaker, Greenlees and Sons Ltd, boot and shoemakers – whose sign advertises 'Repairs neatly done' – and D. Campbell's Kinloch Bar on the corner. On the left there is a chemist's, Frank Clifford's Consulting Rooms, a ladies' and gentlemen's hair saloon, and an agent for Perth Dye Works.

An unusual view of Union Street, looking towards Mafeking Place and the Co-op buildings, taken from Cross Street around 1905. The shop fronts include (on the left) Robert McGeachy's ironmonger's, advertised in a contemporary guidebook as stocking enamelled pails and baths, lamps and oils, cycle goods, sporting cartridges, golf balls and 'cardboard boxes for sending game and eggs by parcel post'. Further down are H.H. Taylor's dental consulting rooms and, on the right, at 2–4 Union Street are James McMurchy's tearooms and baker's. His bill of fare included tea, coffee or cocoa at 2d for a small cup or 3d for a large one, a plate of boiled ham for 4d, a mutton pie or a poached egg and toast for 2d, and a buttered scone or a slice of bread and butter for a penny.

Campbeltown Cross is a fine example of a mediaeval Celtic cross in the Iona style of carving. The Latin inscription on it commemorates Andrew MacEachern, rector at Kilkivan in the fourteenth century. It is shown here in its original position in the centre of Main Street, where it was placed for use as the market cross some time after the burgh was founded in 1609. It used to be the focal point for New Year celebrations, and all the Kintyre milestones were measured from there. The drinking fountain in front would have been essential when not all houses in the town had running water. It was – and remains – the custom that funeral processions had to pass the cross. It was removed for safety during the Second World War and stored at Kilkerran Cemetery. It was then re-sited near the Old Quay where it still stands, although the weather and salt air have badly eroded the carvings.

This view looking up Longrow was taken around 1910 and includes groups of children going to school with their schoolbags on their backs. The curved building on the left, occupied at the time of the photograph by a draper, tobacconist and saddler, was once an apothecary's where the renowned artist William McTaggart once worked. The building later became the premises of a painter and decorator's business. Mafeking Place on the right, where the author of this book was born, housed Mathews' furniture and upholstery store. In 1907 the business advertised its 'immense stock of everything in the house furnishing line, too numerous to mention', and its services as a 'removal contractor by land and sea'.

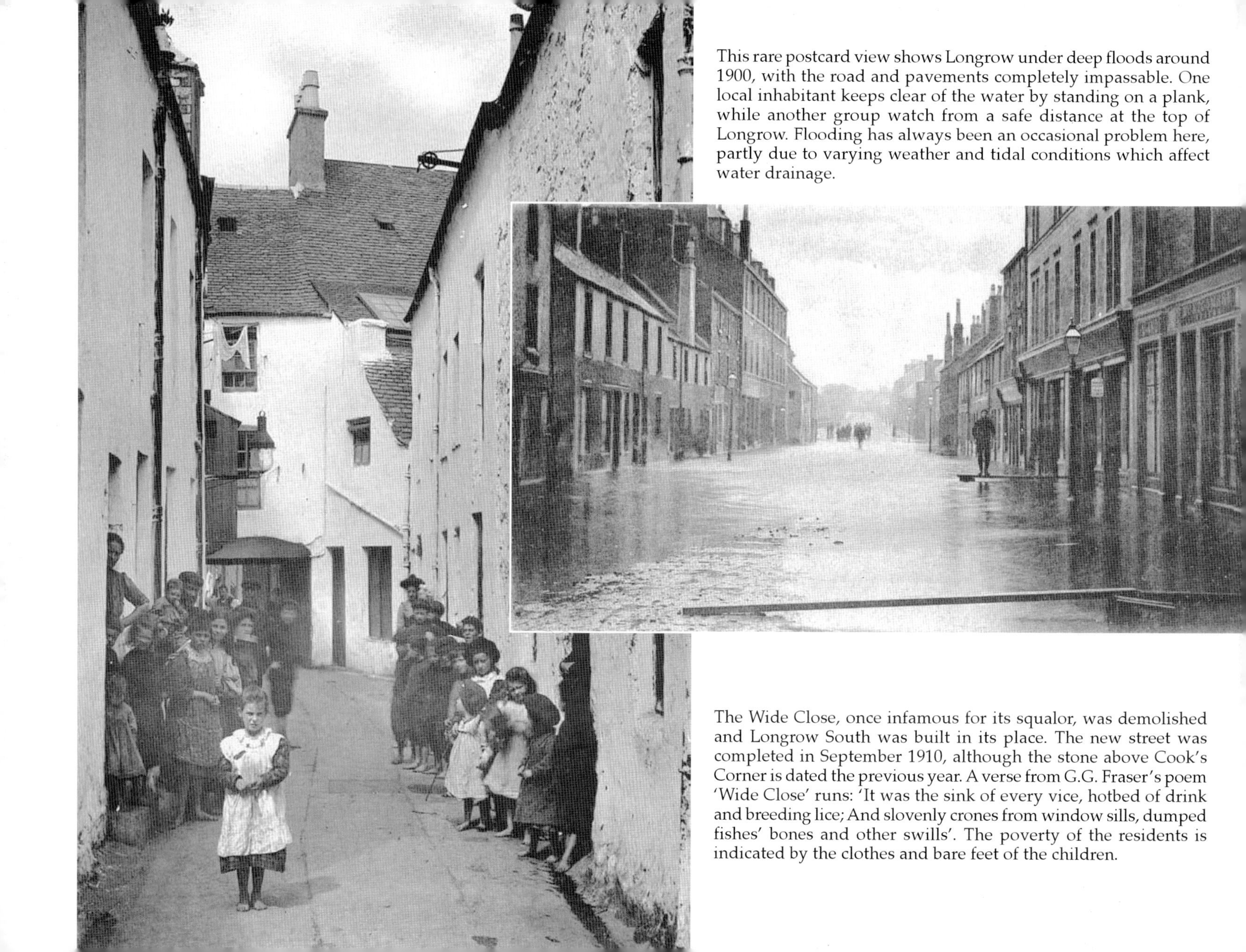

This rare postcard view shows Longrow under deep floods around 1900, with the road and pavements completely impassable. One local inhabitant keeps clear of the water by standing on a plank, while another group watch from a safe distance at the top of Longrow. Flooding has always been an occasional problem here, partly due to varying weather and tidal conditions which affect water drainage.

The Wide Close, once infamous for its squalor, was demolished and Longrow South was built in its place. The new street was completed in September 1910, although the stone above Cook's Corner is dated the previous year. A verse from G.G. Fraser's poem 'Wide Close' runs: 'It was the sink of every vice, hotbed of drink and breeding lice; And slovenly crones from window sills, dumped fishes' bones and other swills'. The poverty of the residents is indicated by the clothes and bare feet of the children.

This Edwardian postcard view shows the newly built Longrow South, with Longrow beyond. The photographer attracted a crowd of local boys, many of whom have their heads covered but their feet bare, and the lad on the right is probably delivering milk. Shops and businesses of the day included the Kinloch Bar, McGown's fish shop, and Stalker's saddlers. The postcard, sent in 1910, carries the message: 'I'm sending you this that you may see the new street, lately opened up. The shops have quite a city look about them, McEwing's, J.M. Brown's china shop and the Herald office.'

Campbeltown Grammar School, pictured around 1900. Built in 1792, it was extended in 1876 to accommodate 300 pupils, both boys and girls. The large tree was once part of a tree-lined avenue from Limecraigs House. The wall on the left of the picture is now part of the entrance to the health centre which was built in 1981/82; the tree was cut down around ten years later. The school building is now the Community Education Centre, which houses Argyll College for Further Education.

This comprehensive view of the town, looking eastwards over Glebe Street towards the loch and Davaar Island, was taken from Gallowhill on a long-gone summer's day. The steeple of what was then Longrow Church (now the Lorne and Lowland Church), dominates the townscape, and across the loch a ship can be seen on the stocks at Trench Point shipyard. At one time Campbeltown had more than thirty distilleries, and rows of distillery buildings (including the chimney of Springbank Distillery) can be seen behind the hay rucks.

Dalintober folk used to see themselves as being separate from the rest of Campbeltown. Net-drying poles belonging to the Dalintober fishermen can be seen on the shore, and on the right of the photograph, two or three of the Dalintober skiffs can just be made out moored offshore in the loch. The men are wheeling a net barrow, which was used for transporting nets and other gear, and also to sell surplus fish when other markets were exhausted. The whitewashed building on the left was a store for fishing nets and was struck by a German incendiary bomb on 9 February 1941, causing the roof to catch fire. It was never repaired and the building was demolished the following year, leaving a gap site which has only recently been taken over by a garage.

Local boys taking part in a model yacht race in Dalintober around 1900. The boy in the lead is thought to be Henry Martin, a Dalintober fisherman's son who himself became a fisherman and died in 1981 at the age of 90. The houses pictured on the left have since been demolished and the site is now occupied by Campbeltown Yachting Club. At the extreme right and left of the photograph, on the shore, can be seen the fishermen's net-drying poles or 'stances' as they were known.

A fine photograph from around 1904, showing one of the Loch Fyne skiffs, William Cook's *Enterprise*, under full sail in Campbeltown Loch with Dalintober in the background. The Loch Fyne skiff had a distinctive slope to its mast, which was set far forward to give the fishermen space in the middle of the boat to haul in their catch. They varied from 32 ft to 37 ft long, with a few as long as 40 ft, and three long oars or 'sweeps' were used when the wind dropped.

The eternal fascination of boys with boats can be seen in this postcard of the slipway in front of the Victoria Hall, looking north across the head of the loch to Dalintober with Knock Scalbert in the background being the highest point. Dalintober Distillery, popularly known as 'the Tin Still', is on the left. It closed down in 1925 after a working life of almost a hundred years.

A busy scene on the Old Quay around 1910, with one of the turbine steamers (probably the *Queen Alexandra*) letting off her passengers. In the foreground are two horse-drawn brakes and a cart being loaded with cargo from a visiting schooner. To the right of the schooner is an East Coast drift-netter, almost certainly a 'bauldie', with Leith as its port of registration. In the background are the houses of High and Low Askomil, and the Dalintober fishing fleet can be seen at anchor.

This atmospheric photograph of the Old Quay comes from the magnificent MacGrory collection of around 3,000 glass negatives, which were taken by Charles and Denis MacGrory in the early 1900s. The photographers were the father and uncle of the late A.P. MacGrory, former provost of Campbeltown, who preserved the collection and donated it to Argyll & Bute Library Services so that future generations could enjoy it. The images form a unique time capsule of Campbeltown and district at the time, and many have already been printed and exhibited, with work going on to process many more. The schooner on the right is the *Star o' Doon*.

Fishing was one of the mainstays of the Campbeltown economy from the eighteenth century onwards. By the 1920s, when this photograph of the herring fleet moored in the inner harbour was taken, ring-netting (a two-boat operation to encircle a shoal of fish) had taken the place of drift-netting (a string of nets suspended from the surface, into which herring swim and become enmeshed). The deck layout on these Loch Fyne skiffs can be seen, and although motor power was by then generally in use, sails were still carried for auxiliary purposes. The crews are beginning to assemble before the evening departure to the herring-fishing grounds.

The Old Quay was still a busy place in the early 1920s, with a mixture of steam and sailing ships. Around thirty or forty fishing skiffs can be seen on the right, with a schooner in front of them. A topsail schooner and an early puffer are tied up on the left and the steamer behind them is probably the *Kinloch*, which went out of service in 1926. The barrels would have been full of salted herring for markets in Glasgow and elsewhere.

By the early 1950s lorries had taken over from horse-drawn carts and, in the left background, a mechanical coal chute had been installed. A Royal Navy ship, probably a frigate, is tied up at the end of the quay. The huts in the middle of the quay were manned to collect pier dues from steamer passengers. At the New Quay, the Campbeltown lifeboat can be made out along with a Navy submarine and three of James O'Hara's punts which were hired out to locals or tourists. The fishing boat CN142, berthed in the corner, is Baldy Stewart's *Boy Danny*, launched at St Monans in July 1948, and the *Pibroch* was a puffer which mainly carried whisky. In the foreground, Angus McGougan, in his working gear, stands beside his coal lorry, while two old men watch the world go by as they take their ease on upended fish-boxes.

There were obviously plenty of willing helpers ready with advice to coax this horse on to the S.S. *Davaar*, whose sister ships were the *Kinloch* and the *Kintyre*. The boxes in the foreground contained fish destined for Glasgow. This postcard was addressed in 1910 to Dan Black, fishing skiff *May Queen*, 454 CN, Stranraer, and the message from his daughter ran: 'Dear Father, we got the money alright last Saturday and are pleased to hear that you've had another fishing this week. We are all well at home and hope you are well. Mother sent clothes with the *Pirate* [a Glasgow cargo-steamer] on Wednesday night. Nancy and Duncan got the P.C.'s you sent. Duncan wanted his to the school to show to his teacher. James had 50 baskets last Saturday morning and we've all had to go into a corner ever since. The weather is very stormy here just now. With love from all, Bella.'

The crowded Old Quay in the early 1950s, the arrival of one of the regular steamers always being a main event of the day. A row of buses can be seen waiting to take visitors on a short trip to Machrihanish or Southend before they went back on board. The large fleet of ring-net fishing boats are tied up in the inner harbour while local boys on the stern of a boat in the bottom left fish for young saithe or 'cuddies'. The Calton 'prefabs' can be seen in the background to the left of Lochend Church steeple.

A fresh catch of herring was salted and packed in barrels as part of the curing process before they were sent off to Glasgow and further afield. Will Douglas, pictured centre with a small boy, began business as a buyer of rabbits before becoming a fish-buyer. He rented Knockbay Farm, choosing it in preference to Hillside so that he could see the fishing fleet coming in. This gave him time to harness his pony and trap so that he could be on the quayside before his competitors. The nets used by the fishermen would have been made locally, with net factories established from the mid-nineteenth century until the last one, Flaws and Shaw, closed in 1986 when the partners retired. The masts of the fishing skiffs reach above the north side of the Old Quay.

This evocative postcard photograph, entitled 'The Morning's Catch', dates back to around 1910 and shows women on the Old Quay gutting the herring and packing them into barrels. The women (many of whom travelled from fishing ports on the east coast of Scotland) are gutting the fish round a large container known as a 'farlan'. Campbeltown was not a major herring-curing port in the late nineteenth and early twentieth centuries, because by then the local fleet was concentrating on ring-netting which supplied a fresh market, rather than drift-netting which was mainly for a curing market. Commercial herring-curing ended here in the mid-1930s.

Fishermen and fishing skiffs (including the *Valkyrie*, owned by McKinlay of Dalintober, on the left) are shown in this image of the New Quay-head with Robert Wylie's boatyard pictured on the right. The yard built many fine skiffs and the last boat launched from here was the *Gratitude* in 1936. The distinctive figurehead above the door was salvaged from the clipper *Charlemagne* which was wrecked in fog at Feochaig on 19 March 1857 while on her maiden voyage. The building on the left was the original lifeboat shed until a replacement was built in 1898 at the opposite end of Quarry Green. The Highland Parish Church can be seen in the background at the top of New Quay Street.

The sight of a submarine in Campbeltown Loch, with its complement of naval personnel on deck, would have caused a lot of interest in the town. The message on the back of the postcard said, 'H.M. Submarine H47 returning to Campbeltown Harbour after a day's diving and torpedo attacks.'

This photograph, another example of the MacGrory brothers' camera work, shows the Royal Navy torpedo boat No. 13 after it ran aground on the shores of the loch. This type of boat was capable of 26 knots, was armed with two 12 lb guns and three torpedo tubes, and had a crew of 39. No. 13 went on to serve in the First World War. The vessel is ashore off Glenramskill and NATO oil tanks now occupy part of the hillside to the right of the picture. The stretch of woodland above the road is known as the 'Wee Wud'.

British naval training ships called in to Campbeltown from time to time with their crews of young sailors. HMS *Northampton* visited in June 1903, and several postcards such as this exist, recording the event as the young 'blue jackets' disembarked and marched through the town. They took part in a sports day (in a field loaned by Captain Duncan Stewart, R.N.), which included gymnastics, races and a tug o' war.

Davaar Island, which can be reached at low tide by crossing the Doirlinn tidal sandbar, pictured from Kilkerran. A cave on the island is home to a painting of the Crucifixion, which was created by the artist Archibald Mackinnon in 1887. Time and weather have gradually eroded the painting, although it has been restored by successive local artists. Davaar lighthouse was built in 1854, prior to which a light was displayed in Kilkerran Cottage for the benefit of mariners.

A topsail schooner, silhouetted in the loch at sunrise, with a Loch Fyne skiff in the foreground. The photograph looks south-east towards the Lodan, the once-prolific fishing ground which lies between Davaar Island and Auchenhoan Head. The message on the back of the postcard, sent in July 1904, reads: 'Hat arrived safe. I am Delighted with it, writing tomorrow. Lizzie is getting her Holidays next week, going to Glasgow with Mary.'

A crowd of spectators watch the flooding at the head of the Old Quay and surrounding streets in January 1915. Frequent flooding, particularly at the head of Longrow and at Lochend, has become a greater problem than ever before due to new sewage pipes which were laid a few years ago.

Campbeltown Bowling Club, popularly known as Stronvaar Bowling Club, was opened in 1906 to satisfy the growing demand for space as the membership of the existing Argyll Bowling Club increased to overflowing. When Argyll Bowling Club started up in 1876, a report in the *Campbeltown Courier* on 6 May said: 'This fine bowling green, situated at the head of the Longrow, which has been laid out by our Good Templar brethren at considerable labour and expense, will be opened today at 3 p.m. The juvenile brass band in connection with the Lodge will be present at the opening and discourse some pieces of music while the play is proceeding.' The Templars' Hall at Millknowe was demolished in June 2003.

A busy scene around the Old Mill which – apart from being a popular playground for local youngsters – was used to grind grain brought in by farmers, with oats probably being the main crop which was milled into oatmeal. Although the dam itself is long gone, the Mill Dam is still referred to, and Millknowe, Mill Road, Mill Street and Millers Park all commemorate the spot. It probably closed down in the early 1930s and the building and surrounding lands were acquired by the council in 1937 for housing development.

Millknowe Street, with the two-storey houses of Millknowe Terrace behind, is the first street visitors see when they drive into Campbeltown from the Tarbert road. The terrace was the first housing project of Campbeltown Building Company, which was founded in 1877 to 'provide suitable accommodation for the working classes'. Each house had a room, kitchen, and 'lighted bed closet', and there was an outside toilet which was shared between every two units. One of the young women has her baby snugly wrapped inside her tartan 'plyde', or shawl.

Peter MacKay's patent rick-lifter did away with the time-consuming and skilled job of building hay onto carts. The inventor was born around 1838 at the Learside farm of Erradill. The prototype was tried out by John Douglas on Christlach Farm, Southend, in September 1888, and a year later more than 150 of MacKay's rick-lifters were in use throughout Scotland.

This postcard was issued to commemorate the Campbeltown men who carried out a heroic rescue of the crew of the ketch *Jane* of Belfast, which foundered opposite Dalintober Quay in a severe blizzard on 29 December 1908. They braved a snowstorm to save the lives of two young men who had lashed themselves to the mast of their vessel all night in the loch, although their father, Captain Houston, died from exposure. The volunteer crew were (back row, from left) D. Morrans, Hugh McLean, Archibald Blair, Tom McArthur; and (front, from left) J. Meenan, Captain Duncan Martin, and James McLean. The men are wearing distinctively patterned fishermen's jerseys, which were hand-knitted in oiled wool to protect them against the elements.

The narrow-gauge Campbeltown & Machrihanish Light Railway started in August 1906 and from the outset it was a popular attraction for locals and visitors alike, carrying 10,000 passengers in the first three weeks alone. One of the steam locomotives is pictured with its three carriages leaving the quay-head terminus and travelling along Hall Street at the start of its journey to Machrihanish. In the background are the flats in Royal Avenue Mansions, designed by Frank Burnet and Boston of Glasgow, and the selection of shops on the ground level include John Scott's Clothier and Ladies' Tailor, and a laundry. The small wooden building at that time was the Argyll Photographic Studio.

Seen on the start of its journey, the train is passing alongside Quarry Green which had yet to be built up as it is still without pavements or railings. The locomotives *Argyll* and *Atlantic* pulled their distinctive low carriages to Machrihanish, where the track ran behind the villas to stop at the wooden station at the back of the old Mission Hall. The railway service closed in 1932.

The train's route along Hall Street passed the Free Library, which was opened at the end of 1898, thanks to the generosity of landowner James Macalister Hall of Killean who gifted it to the town. Now an A-listed building, it was designed by John James Burnet, in what he called the 'Scots Renaissence' style. It also incorporates a museum which drew most of its early artefacts from the collection of the Kintyre Scientific Association, founded in 1890. A garden in memory of Linda McCartney has been created in the library grounds.

The carriages of the 'wee train', with C&MLR painted on the side, at the terminus on Hall Street, *c*.1910. In the background can be seen the single-storey weigh-house, or 'wee'us', used to weigh heavy loads being shipped in or out of the Old Quay and one of the main gathering places of retired fishermen and seamen. Sadly, it was demolished more than thirty years ago. Behind the early motor car is the Royal Hotel which sustained a direct hit by an enemy bomb during the Second World War. In the background, nets are drying on Kinloch Green.

The locomotive *Argyll* and its carriages, surrounded by a curious crowd of barefoot boys at the quay-head terminus in Hall Street. Unlike most other train systems, the Light Railway did not run on fenced-off, privately designated tracks. Bad weather occasionally caused disruption, with a storm in 1915 covering the tracks on Quarry Green with debris. The storm also caused Machrihanish Water to burst its banks, flooding the railway and putting out the fire in the locomotive which became stranded.

Ladies in Edwardian dress, about to board the train at the terminus. An advert in a local guidebook of 1907 announced: 'Frequent Trains run between Campbeltown and Machrihanish Golf Links. Time occupied, Twenty minutes. Return fare, 1/-. Season Tickets for Fourteen days and upwards issued at Greatly Reduced Rates. Special Trains can be arranged for on Moderate Terms. Alex Black, Superintendent, Railway Office, Campbeltown.'

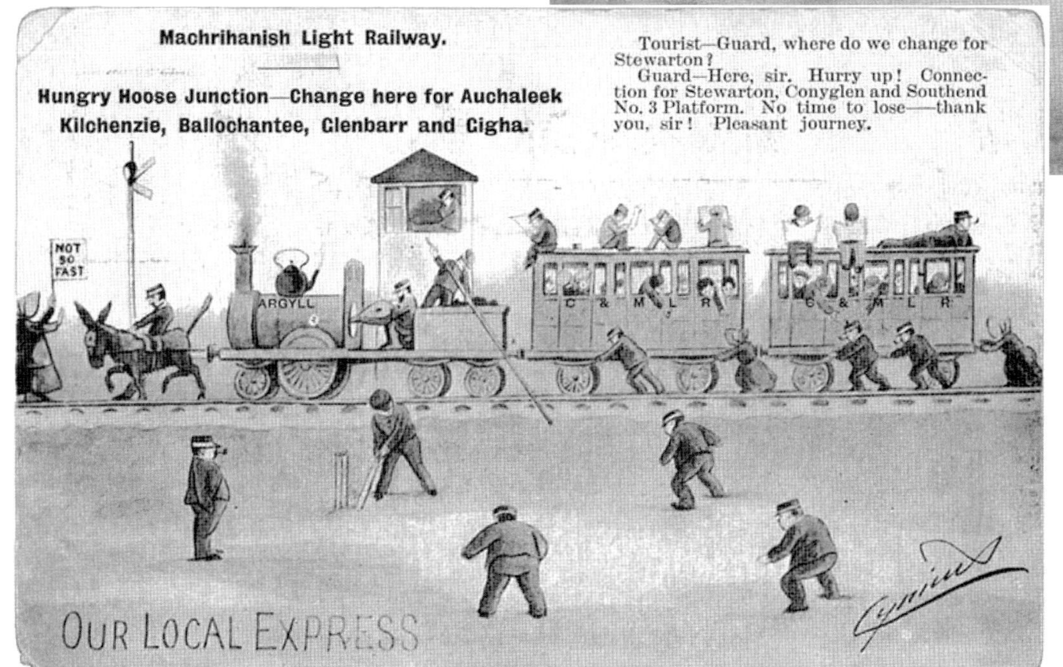

A comic postcard, issued at the time the 'wee train' was in service. The artist Cynicus supplied his drawings to illustrate other railways in other locations, and incorporated different captions around the image of the train and personnel.

This was the original old village at Machrihanish, known as the Pans or Saltpans because of the salt-making industry which was carried on there in the seventeenth and eighteenth centuries. The buildings included (from left) Lossit Gatehouse (the only one still standing), a row of red-roofed cottages known as the 'Rid Ra', and a smiddy at the back which closed down around 1920. The old inn on the right of the picture was thought to have been built as a private house in the late eighteenth century by Charles McDowall of Cricken, who had a lease of the salt pans and the coal pit at Drumlemble. It was taken over and used as an inn by the Rae family from Aberdeenshire, who were salmon and lobster fishermen, but it fell into disrepair after 1877 when a new inn was built on the site where the Ugadale Arms Hotel now stands.

This photograph, taken from the grassy knoll known as the Duan, shows the villas and the Mission Hall at the west end of Machrihanish, with a horse tied up outside Livingstone's general store. In 1907 Miss Livingstone advertised her business as stocking 'groceries, provisions, confections, aerated waters, fancy goods emporium, local view goods, postcards, newspapers and magazines'. The shop was still open in the 1950s, but the complications of rationing had taken their toll and the only reminders of confectionery by that time were the pre-war Five Boys and Milk Tray chocolate adverts.

The Ugadale Arms Hotel, pictured from the bathing stage which has long since disappeared into the Atlantic waves. The hotel suffered a fire in February 1898, the cause of which was thought to have been sparks from a chimney which ignited the roof. The cost of the damage was £8,000, a huge sum at that time. A report in the *Argyllshire Herald* said: 'When the news spread through Campbeltown about 4 o'clock that the Pans Hotel was on fire and likely to be destroyed, the public excitement ran high and many either hired conveyances or proceeded to the scene on foot while a number of cyclists journeyed to Machrihanish on the ever-popular bicycle. District farmers and others from Stewarton, Southend and the surrounding country also drove to the scene and witnessed the fire at its height.'

The Gauldrons at Machrihanish. There are many theories about the origin of the name, including comparisons with a witch's cauldron because of the constantly moving sea, or the vessels used in salt-making. It can also be argued that it represents, in corrupt form, *gallan-mor*, which is Gaelic for the butterbur, a rhubarb-like plant which grows there. One of William McTaggart's best-known paintings, 'The Coming of St Columba', shows the Gauldrons and he painted several works showing other parts of the Machrihanish shore. Sheep (and sometimes feral goats) still graze freely on the springy turf and it remains one of the most beautiful wild, but accessible, spots in Kintyre. The formation of the beach changes from time to time because of the battering of the waves, and one year's golden sand can be replaced by rock and shingle the following year.

This rare photograph from 1905 shows the Wireless Telegraph Station at the Gauldrons, an early experiment in communications between America and Europe. The Fessenden system had a steel signalling mast 420 ft high, supported by wire ropes, and it successfully transmitted and received simple messages. But just six days before Professor Reginald Fessenden, a Canadian, planned to give a public demonstration of speech across the Atlantic in December 1906, the whole structure was blown down in a gale. The huge concrete blocks which anchored the wires still remain. Many local people at the time believed it was a closely guarded spy system and sixty years later a local booklet, describing it as the 'Mystery Tower', voiced the opinion that: 'The word 'spies' was often whispered and when the VIP personnel connected with it were interned as spies in America during the First World War, it would seem their suspicions were not very wide of the mark.'

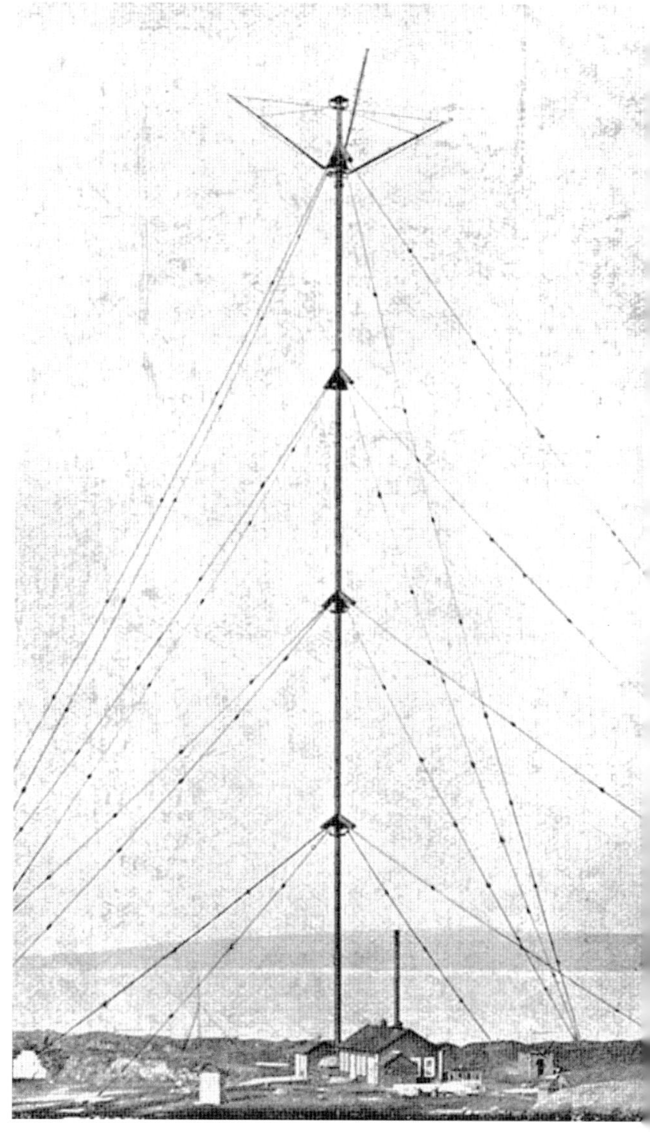

The lifeboat station at Machrihanish was officially opened on 24 August 1912 by Mrs Macneal of Ugadale, while her daughter named the lifeboat *Henry Finlay*. The boat was purchased with a bequest of £1,000, left by Mr Finlay who stipulated that a lifeboat should be named after himself and, if possible, stationed on the south-west coast of Scotland. The ceremony, which was also attended by Provost McMurchy of Campbeltown, took place one day later than planned because of excessive rain on 23 August. Mrs Macneal was presented with a ceremonial key, which she in turn donated to Campbeltown Museum, and her daughter was given a gold badge. Since 1992, the building has been used by Machrihanish Marine Environmental Laboratory.

Machrihanish airfield was used as a quick and convenient way for this group of shepherds to transport their sheepdogs. It's probable that these were Islay shepherds returning home with their dogs after competing in the County Sheepdog Trials in Kintyre. The airport recently celebrated its seventieth anniversary, having opened as a commercial concern in 1933.

The eighteenth hole of Machrihanish golf course. Originally founded as a ten-hole course in 1876, it was upgraded first to 12 holes and then in 1879 to its present 18 holes under the guidance of the legendary Tom Morris of St Andrews, whose first view of the location was accompanied by his historic words: 'Providence meant this for a gowf coorse'. This site is now the practice putting green, with the professional's shop nearby, and the eighteenth green is closer to the road and further east. The ladies' clubhouse can be seen to the left of the Ugadale Arms Hotel, and the men's clubhouse is on the right. The track of the Light Railway ran behind the hotel.

The Backs Water, fed by streams including those which flow from Tirfergus Glen, Uigle Glen and the Black Loch and entering the Atlantic near the southern end of the links, is one of the natural hazards on Machrihanish golf course. Many a golfer has lost a ball in the water, and many local youngsters have fished them out and re-sold them to earn some pocket money. When the club was founded in 1876, by eight local gentlemen who resolved that 'a club should be formed for the purpose of playing golf in the vicinity of Campbeltown', it was originally called the Kintyre Golf Club. In the first year of the club's existence, a gold medal was presented by Captain John Lorne Stewart to be played for annually.

The nine-hole ladies' golf course in Machrihanish runs alongside the highly-regarded 18-hole course laid out beside the shores of the Atlantic. The author's late mother, Nancy Burgess, is pictured on the right of this photograph taken in 1936. The row of villas on the other side of the road were built from the early 1890s onwards.